Who Am I And Why Should You Care?

If you don't know who I am, that's okay.

My name is **Carlos Redlich**. I'm a Florida native who moved to Arizona to enjoy the west.

I've been a copywriter for over 15 years.

I've written million dollar promos, worked with your favorite guru's (and maybe even a few you hate)... and I've been the secret weapon business owners keep in their back pocket when they want a high converting funnel.

Before diving all in into copywriting, I also used to co-own a martial art school where I learned how to teach what I know.

I attended seminars that focused specifically on how to *teach* and transfer complicated information... in a simple way anyone can understand.

<u>Trust me... teaching is a skill that *most* business authors unfortunately never develop.</u>

In fact, a lot of them are good at "the thing" they're trying to teach but *terrible* at transferring that knowledge in a practical way others can benefit from.

It's like the ring fighter that's great at knocking people out but doesn't have the patience to teach others.

Some people are just fighters.
Some are just teachers.
Some can do both.

<u>Fortunately for you, I can do both.</u>

I get in the trenches, break stuff and then figure out how to put it back together.

After I figure it out, I pass on that knowledge to you.

Simple. Easy. Transparent.

Oh and one last thing for the pirates out there...

Copyright © 2023 by Carlos Redlich.
All rights reserved.
No portion of this book may be reproduced in any form without written permission from the publisher or author, except as permitted by U.S. copyright law.

Now turn the page and let's get started...

By Picking Up This Book, You've Uncovered A Treasure Trove Of 20 Marketing And Copywriting Tips

(Start Your Journey On This Page)

Dear Friend,

In this book, you'll be given advice on all things related to marketing, copywriting and more.

What I've done is taken some of the posts I've shared on social media and compiled them into this book.

This way all of the best stuff is organized so it's *easy* for you to get value out of it.

This book is great for your coffee stand because it'll be unlike anything else there.

On top of that, I guarantee that **ANYONE** who simply *skims* through these pages will find something of value.

Anyway, I won't keep you for too much longer…

There's no table of contents, forward or anything else.

We're getting straight to the good stuff so get ready... get set... and *turn* the page!

Tip 1-

Sell high ticket offers and services?

Using an email follow up campaign is critical to your growth as a company.

Here are a few reasons why:

1. It shows that you value your lead and their possible business.

By taking the time to follow up with a potential client, you're showing that you're interested in working with them and value their business. This can help build trust because you're not letting the relationship "fall through the cracks."

2. It helps keep your business top of mind.

In 2022 and especially in 2023, it can be easy for potential clients to forget about a product or service they were interested in. They're distracted by social media, fires in their business and life in general.

By following up with an email, you can remind them of your business and keep it top of mind.

3. It allows you to provide additional information or answer any questions.

   A follow-up email is a great way to provide potential customers with additional information so they can make a proper decision. It's also a chance for them to ask any questions so you can move them closer to making a purchase.

4. It increases the chances of making a sale.

   By following up with leads, you're increasing the chances of making a sale. A well-written and personalized email can help convert interested prospects into paying customers.

I hope this convinces you to email your list more often.

Like I just mentioned earlier, email follow-up is an important part of the sales process.

It shows that you value the customer's business while staying top of mind. It also gives you a higher chance of making a sale. Now go kick some ass!

Tip 2-

Marketing 101...

Marketing is all about persuading potential customers to buy your product or service.

Persuasion is a powerful tool that can help you get your message across and influence people to take action.

Here are a few tips on how to use persuasion in your marketing:

First, it's important to understand the psychology behind persuasion.

People are more likely to be swayed by arguments that appeal to their emotions, rather than those that are purely logical.

Why?

Simple.

It's because emotions drive people's decision-making, and when you can tap into someone's emotions, you can influence their behavior.

One effective way to persuade people is by using social proof.

You see, people are more likely to take action if they see others doing it.

For example, if you have a lot of positive reviews or testimonials from satisfied customers, this can be a powerful way to persuade potential customers to buy your product.

Another effective persuasion technique is to offer a limited-time offer or a sense of urgency.

The thing is, when you do this... it NEEDS to be real.

Otherwise you're asking for the alphabet agencies to knock on your door after you sell a few million dollars worth of stuff.

When people feel like they have to act quickly, they're more likely to take action.

For example, if you're offering a discount on your product, but only for a limited time, this can create a sense of urgency that'll persuade your prospect to buy.

Finally, it's important to be transparent and honest in your marketing efforts.

I know that may sound counter-intuitive to direct marketers, but it's true.

People are more likely to be persuaded by arguments that are honest and straightforward.

If you try to deceive or manipulate people, they're likely to see through it and be less receptive to your message.

And if they do buy, there's a good chance they'll feel used.

And if they feel used, they'll either ask for a refund or simply stop buying from you all together.

Or even worse, they'll humiliate you publicly and report you to the feds.

So don't be a jerk.

Tell the truth.

Long story short, persuasion is a powerful tool that can help you get your message across and convince people to take action.

By understanding the psychology behind persuasion, using social proof, creating a REAL sense of urgency, and being transparent and honest, you can effectively (and ethically) use persuasion in your marketing to make more sales, more often.

Tip 3-

In the age of social media, standing out from the crowd can be a challenge as a business owner.

Especially online.

Consumers are bombarded with advertisements, marketing messages, and sales pitches from businesses of all sizes and industries.

So, how can you grab their attention and get them to take notice of your brand?

One powerful way to connect with your audience and drive more sales is by using *stories* in your marketing.

<u>Stories have the ability to capture the imagination, engage the emotions, and create a sense of connection with your audience.</u>

When done well, stories can be a powerful tool for driving more sales and building a loyal customer base.

How can you use stories in your marketing to make more sales?

EASY!

1- Identify the story you want to tell.

Before you can start using stories in your marketing, you need to know what story you want to tell.

This could be the story of how your business got started, the story of a customer who had a great experience with your product or service, or the story of a problem that your business solved for someone.

2- Use storytelling techniques to capture the attention of your audience.

Once you know the story you want to tell, it's time to start crafting it in a way that will capture the attention of your audience.

This means using storytelling techniques like setting, character development, and conflict to create a compelling narrative that will keep your audience engaged and interested.

3 - Make your story relatable to your audience.

One of the keys to using stories in your marketing is to make them relatable to your audience.

If your audience can't picture themselves as the main character or at least emphasize with them, they'll stop reading.

Here's how you can make your story more relatable...

Use examples and scenarios that your audience can easily identify with so it connects with their emotions and experiences.

4- Use your story to showcase the benefits of your product or service.

A great story can help to showcase the benefits of your product or service in a way that's memorable.

By highlighting how your product or service was the savior in someone's life, you can create a sense of value.

It also demonstrates why your audience should consider buying from you.

Here's a fake story to give you an example...

Years ago, there was a young man named Tony who had a dream of starting his own business.

He had always been entrepreneurial as a child and had a passion for creating and building things.

So, when he graduated from college, he decided to take the plunge and start his own company.

At first, it was a struggle.

Tony had no experience running a business and didn't know how to get things off the ground.

He spent countless hours researching, networking, and trying to drum up business.

But no matter how hard he tried, it seemed like nothing was working.

Despite the challenges, Tony was determined to make his business succeed.

He knew he had a great product and a solid business plan, and he wasn't going to give up.

So, he continued to put in the hard work and long hours, never losing sight of his goal.

Slowly but surely, things started to turn around for Tony.

He found the XYZ mentorship and used the strategies he was shown to grow his business quickly.

Shortly after joining the mentorship, he landed his first few clients and began to build a loyal customer base.

As word of his business spread, more and more people started to take notice.

And as the years went on, Tony's business continued to grow and thrive.

He added new products and services, expanded into new markets, and even opened a second location.

And before he knew it, he had achieved the success he had always dreamed of.

Looking back, Tony realized that starting his own business had been one of the most challenging and rewarding experiences of his life.

It wasn't easy, but because of what he was shown in the xyz mentorship, he was able to become the success he always dreamed he could be.

His hard work and determination had paid off in the end.

He was proud of what he had accomplished and grateful for the many opportunities that had come his way.

And that, my friends, is the story of how one young man's dream became a reality.

It just goes to show that with hard work, perseverance, and a little bit of mentorship, anything is possible.

The end.

As you can see, using stories in your marketing can be a powerful way to connect with your audience and drive more sales.

And it's the best way to differentiate your company while "humanizing" it at the same time.

Tip 4-

Are you pre-qualifying leads in your sales process?

I'd only really suggest a pre-qualification step if you're getting a lot of leads.

If you're only getting a small handful, you just need more time on the phone to figure out how to market to them better.

But let's say you are getting a lot of leads but your closers aren't closing a lot of them.

It might be the closers fault but as marketers, what can we do to improve the flow of leads coming in?

One thing you can do is have leads watch some kind of video that tells them about what you do and then ask them to book a call if they meet certain criteria.

You'll want some kind of follow up campaign in place to make sure people actually watch the video.

Again, I'm only really suggesting this if you're getting a lot of leads.

If you're getting on five calls per week for example and closing one or two deals a month, you just need more leads at this point.

Or to increase your prices… but that's another topic for another day.

When you implement something like a video sales letter that leads have to watch before booking a call, you save time for your sales people so they're only focused on closing qualified leads.

The rest of the time they can focus on doing follow up calls, texts and emails with past deals that haven't gone through yet.

Plus, if someone gets on a call with you or your sales person after watching a video that explains what you do and gives testimonials / proof…

… then your sales call will typically be shorter and your close rates should go up because it's almost like taking an order, if the video script is done right.

Tip 5-

Want to scale your offer?

After working with over 500 clients in almost every niche and industry imaginable…

Here's a few things you'll want to keep in mind:

1- Focus on customer acquisition and retention:

When you're just launching, I'd suggest focusing the majority of your effort on acquiring front end customers.

I'd recommend pushing people into subscription offers as well as high ticket.

High ticket offers can make you a lot of money but having some kind of subscription in place can keep the cash flow coming in if people stop qualifying for loans or some kind of recession hits and money gets tighter for folks.

2- Invest in technology and infrastructure:

I'm not a technology guru but a lot of the best clients I've worked with invest in their tech stack.

If you've got a winning team in place but a shitty race car, you won't go far.

The vehicle you're in is important (I'm using an analogy here people).

But if you have a great "car" and a great team, plus a great offer, you will have a great chance at success.

3- Continuously innovate and improve:

This may seem obvious but it isn't something a majority of biz owners tend to think about from my experience.

To stay ahead of the competition, it's important to continuously innovate and improve the business.

That could mean creating a new offer, improving the old one, finding holes in your business to patch up, improving customer service and deliverability, etc.

Listen, growing a business isn't easy but if you focus on the right stuff it can be easier.

Good luck and kick some ass!

Tip 6-

If your revenue relies on persuasion... pay close attention and take some notes.

I'm about to reveal a few key secrets you can harness for maximum results in your marketing.

Secret #1- Know your audience:

Obviously, it's important to understand the needs, values, and motivations of the people you're trying to persuade.

If you don't have a perfect message-to-market match, you won't be nearly as effective.

Secret #2- Use logic and evidence:

People are more likely to be persuaded by arguments that are supported by logical reasoning and evidence.

That's why it's important to make your sales arguments clear while using facts and data to support your claims.

Secret #3- Appeal to emotions:

While logic and evidence are important, you're not a good marketer until you recognize that people are emotional beings and that emotional appeals can be very powerful in persuasion.

Try to appeal to the emotions of your audience by using stories, examples, and analogies that they can relate to.

It's an easy way to engage their feelings.

Secret #4- Build credibility:

People are more likely to be persuaded by someone who they believe is trustworthy and knowledgeable about the topic at hand.

Build your credibility by getting on podcasts, being featured in online or offline trade publications, etc.

Shockingly... if you're marketing to marketers... you'll also gain a lot of credibility just for being honest and transparent in your arguments.

Crazy, I know...

Secret #5- Use storytelling:

Like I mentioned earlier...

Stories can be a very effective way to persuade people, because it taps into your audience's emotions and makes complex ideas more relatable and understandable.

Use storytelling to help illustrate your points and make them more memorable.

Bonus Secret- Use positive language:

People are generally more receptive to messages that are framed in a positive way.

Instead of focusing on the negative aspects of an issue, try to present your ideas in a positive light and focus on the benefits your customer/client will get.

Apply the secrets to your marketing and watch as your sales effortlessly start to increase.

Tip 7- This Is A Sales Pitch

Are you tired of constantly chasing leads and struggling to get booked calls?

I know a lot of my clients were, until they discovered the power of video sales letters.

VSLs are a great way to qualify leads and get more booked calls.

They allow you to clearly and effectively communicate the value of what you're selling, while also showcasing your personality, expertise and credibility.

If you're interested in having me write you a killer video sales letter, just let me know!

My team can also build out the funnel for you so it's all automated.

My clients have successfully used this strategy to get booked calls for...

- Their coaching business

- Their SaaS offer

- To sell Real Estate

- And tons more!

Don't let another day go by without taking control of your sales process.

Try a VSL with me and watch your booked calls skyrocket in the new year!

Email me at: TheCopyCloser with the subject line: *I want to hire you for a VSL Carlos*

Tip 8-

Copywriting is the missing ingredient your offer needs to scale over the long term.

Here's 2 rules of thumb you can use when writing or critiquing your next piece of copy:

1. **So What?**

    This question helps you make sure your copy is relevant by constantly asking "So what?" at each step.

    On top of that, you'll be able to identify the most important information and cut out any unnecessary "fat".

2. **The Rule of Three**

    This little rule of thumb helps make your copy memorable.

    And when it's more memorable, it makes your reader more emotional.

    And when they're more emotional… they buy more.

See how I just used the rule of three to describe... *the rule of three.*

I did it with a simple chain of logic that conveys the message...

"If customers are emotional, they're more likely to buy" ... but instead of just saying that... I applied the rule of three to make the point more impactful.

You can also do this by describing a product or service in 3 different ways.

At the end of the day, sentences that are presented in threes are more effective and memorable.

Listen, there's tons of copywriting formulas out there, but these two here are easy to remember and even *easier* to apply.

I hope this helps.

Tip 9 -

If you're not consistently testing your marketing campaigns, you're leaving money on the table.

Some of the first things I look at when critiquing copy are…

■ Headlines

■ Images

■ The call to action

■ Placement of the buy buttons

■ The actual offer

■ And the format the marketing is being delivered in

All of these things are important.

The most important in my opinion is the offer because without a great offer, you're not going to sell very much regardless of how much attention you're getting.

But if you do have a great offer, you want to pay attention to all of these different elements because tweaking them even slightly can dramatically increase your conversions and bottom line profits.

Tip 10 -

Every year that goes by, there's a good chance that your audience is getting savvier to past marketing methods.

Particularly really hype ones.

What's the solution?

Be more authentic and transparent.

It helps build trust and credibility with your audience.

It also helps you connect with them on a deeper level if they're similar to you or they admire what you're doing.

When your marketing is authentic, it means that you're being genuine and transparent about your brand, products, services and sometimes... even your personal life.

As long as the intention is uplifting, positive or inspiring, it's not a bad idea to include it somewhere in your marketing.

A lot of people drop the ball here and confuse this with just airing out their baggage and issues.

I don't suggest being that person but that's up to you, boo boo.

Sharing personal experiences brings people closer to you and your world.

Like a filmed wedding proposal or family trips.

This creates a connection with your audience and makes them more likely to engage with your brand overall.

Tip 11-

A headline is the first thing your prospects will see and it can either lure them to keep going through your funnel or turn them away.

Here are some tips for using headlines:

- **Make it catchy:** A headline should be attention-grabbing and compelling, so think about using power words or making a bold statement.

- **Keep it short and sweet:** Most of the headlines that have worked best for me are around 6-12 words.

- **Use action verbs:** Action verbs can help make your headlines more dynamic and push readers to take action.

- **Use numbers:** Lists or headlines that include numbers usually perform well because they give readers a clear idea of what to expect and can be easier to scan for the skimmers.

- **Make it relevant:** The headline should be closely related to the content of the VSL or landing page. If you lure someone in with a catchy headline but don't deliver on it in the body copy, your prospect will lose faith in you because you basically bait and switched them.

Remember, these are tips, not rules.

Can you have a super long headline that works?

Yes.

These are just simple tips you can use if you're just starting out or need to come up with a headline quickly.

Again, the purpose of your headline is to grab attention and get readers to keep reading and going through your sales funnel, so it's important to put some thought into crafting a strong one. not

Can you have a super long headline that works?

Yes.

These are just simple tips you can use if you're just starting out or need to come up with a headline quickly.

Tip 12 -

Want to get more conversions from your offer?

If you've already got an offer that's converting, try improving the guarantee.

There's a good chance that could help it convert even more.

Pretty much everyone knows what a guarantee is but for the newer marketers here's a quick breakdown...

A guarantee is a promise that a company makes to its customers about the quality or satisfaction of its products or services.

Here are some tips for using guarantees in your marketing:

1. **Make it clear:** Make sure that your guarantee is easy for customers to understand and that it covers the most important aspects of your product or service. As the old saying goes, "A confused mind never buys."

2. **Make it relevant:** A guarantee doesn't always have to be a money back one.

   It should be relevant to the needs and concerns of your target audience.

   For example, if you're selling a digital product, service or coaching offer, getting their money back is cool but your client really wants the result you promised.

   In this case you can use a guarantee that states you'll stick with someone until they get a specific result.

3. **Make it specific:** A guarantee that is too vague or general won't work. Instead, make your guarantee specific so it's easy to understand and doesn't seem like you're trying to pull a fast one over their heads.

4. **Make it visible:** Your guarantee should be prominently displayed on your landing page, VSL, packaging, and all marketing materials so that customers can easily find it.

Overall, using a guarantee in your marketing can be a great way to differentiate yourself from competitors while also telling your customers/clients that you've got their back no matter what happens.

When the risk of buying is removed... you get more sales.

Tip 13 -

As a freelance copywriter, there are a few things you can do to gain momentum in your business:

1. **Build a strong portfolio:** Make sure to showcase your best work in your portfolio but also make sure you're not just sending a huge google drive to clients. Sending specific examples is better because it's more relevant to the client and also won't take hours to go through.

2. **Network and market yourself:** Attend events, join mentorships, and do your best to establish yourself as an authority in this space. The secret is consistency and time. If you consistently put out good content and are seen by your prospects repeatedly either through social media, by going to events or through ads, you'll become an authority.

   The *faster* you do this, the better.

3. **Offer excellent customer service:** Make sure to deliver high-quality work on time and communicate with your clients to build a good reputation and attract repeat business. And if your copy doesn't convert... offer to fix

it for free! Don't just take the money and disappear!

4. **Keep learning and improving:** Stay up to date with trends and new technology. AI is a big thing nowadays so if you're not using it to get new ideas, research and help you as a writer, you're ignoring a tool that won't disappear any time soon. Stay ahead of the curve.

At the end of the day, growing a freelance business means you need to consistently market yourself and work closely with clients to make sure their offer converts.

Tip 14-

Use emails in your marketing and want a better click-through rate?

Pay Attention!

One of the things you can do is make your links an image or graphic of some kind because it will typically improve click through rate up to 5X.

The problem I've noticed is if I do this too much, my emails end up in the promotions folder so I usually just do it sporadically.

Tip 15-

Use video sales letters in your marketing?

Read this before writing or launching your next one!

At bare minimum, there's 3 things you need to be aware of when crafting your VSL.

Thing #1 is Audience - This seems basic but without knowing EXACTLY who you're writing to, you won't be able to deliver a hard-hitting script that appeals to your customers' deep emotions and wants.

Thing #2 is Structure - There's a lot of different structures out there in internet-land showing you how to write a VSL. The important part is just picking a single structure and going with that. When you try to combine a bunch of different formulas, approaches and structures into one, it usually doesn't work. Simple is better most of the time.

And finally…

Thing #3 is the most obvious of all… it's having a clear Call To Action - If you're not telling your prospect EXACTLY how to order and what to expect in a clear and concise way... you will lose sales. A confused mind, never buys.

I LOVE using VSLs to get more booked calls so if you're closing deals by appointment, do yourself a favor and test a "book a call funnel" that includes a short VSL (10-15 minutes).

Tip 16 -

When you're trying to think of a Big Idea for your offer, you want to make sure it's relevant to the target audience.

For example, one of my latest facebook posts offering a training on how I use AI and Chat GPT seems to have really resonated with my audience.

That's why it's working on such a simple level (facebook post + paypal link).

One formula for coming up with a big idea in marketing is:

Big Idea = Target Audience + Unique Value Proposition + Emotional Appeal

- **Target Audience:** This is the group of people that your offer is trying to reach. Write down their needs, interests, and values when coming up with a big idea.

- **Unique Value Proposition:** This is the unique benefit or value you offer to the target audience that can't be found anywhere else. One example could be a special guarantee.

- **Emotional Appeal:** This is the emotional connection that you want the offer to create with your target audience. It could be a feeling of joy, nostalgia, security, fear or any other emotion that's relevant to the offer.

With these three elements, you can create a big idea that resonates with your target audience and makes them want to buy.

Tip 17-

Want to know the secret to writing an offer your customers can't refuse?

Well, let me tell you, it breaks down into 8 major components.

First things first, you need a good reason for the offer.

Like, why are you giving away the farm?

Is it a special introductory deal or a solution to a problem?

Whatever it is, make sure it makes sense and that you're positioning yourself as a helpful advocate for the customer.

Next up, discounts.

People love a good deal, right?

So, you gotta establish a regular price that seems like a good value.

Show them how much they'll save or how much they'll benefit from the product, compared to the regular price.

And, a 50% introductory discount is always a crowd-pleaser.

Options, options, options.

You gotta give people choices, but not too many that they get overwhelmed.

Give them a low-end price point with one or more higher options to increase your average sale and return on investment.

Payment terms are also important.

Make sure you offer flexible options to accommodate the customer's needs.

And, a strong and credible guarantee can also help to ease any fears they may have.

Scarcity also plays a big role in power-packed offers.

Create a sense of urgency and scarcity by offering a limited time deal or limited availability.

Testimonials are also a big help, they build trust and credibility for your offer.

If your prospect doesn't trust you, they won't buy from you.

Finally, you've gotta make sure you include a clear call to action for the customer to take the next step and take advantage of your offer.

So, that's it in a nutshell.

Follow these 8 major components and you're on your way to creating a power-packed offer that your customers can't resist!

Tip 18-

If you're a business owner or marketer, this might be you...

You're having a tough day.

You're struggling with feelings of discouragement, self-doubt, insecurity and vulnerability.

These negative emotions have been haunting you for a while now and it feels like they just won't go away.

It's no secret that many people are feeling the same way, especially during uncertain times.

You've been thinking a lot about how these toxic emotions are affecting your personal life and also your income.

You know that when you're feeling negatively, you tend to make poorer decisions which can result in financial losses, lost business and even bankruptcies.

Poker players know this well, we call it being on "tilt".

It's scary to think about and you can't help but wonder if you're alone in this.

But what's even scarier is the fact that these negative emotions also have an impact on your physical health.

Scientists say that these emotions can depress your immune system and increase the incidence of fatal diseases among depressed people.

Crazy!

It's a sad reality and it's even more tragic when you think about how these events are so needless, pointless, uncalled for and unnecessary.

After a lot of reflection, you've come to realize that nearly all of the thoughts and feelings that trigger these tragedies are outright lies.

You've come to understand that emotions are triggered by events and your "belief filters" about those events shape your thoughts and emotions.

I first learned this from Clayton Makepeace years ago.

It's important for you to be aware of your own belief filters and to question the thoughts and feelings that come up.

As a marketer, you also realize the importance of understanding the role of emotions in decision-making and purchasing behavior.

You know that many purchases are made to satisfy emotional needs and not just practical ones.

It's important for you to keep this in mind when creating campaigns and messaging.

If you ever have a tough day, just be grateful for the insights and understanding that you've gained.

You're going to try to focus on the positive and keep moving forward.

Now get out there and kick some ass.

Tip 19 -

You might think there's only one way to write a great headline, but that's not true.

In fact, there's a ton of different techniques you can use to make your headlines stand out.

In this post, we're going to talk about three of the most powerful headline techniques out there.

The first technique is Pure Benefit Headlines.

These headlines only show the main benefit a product/service has to offer.

They're great for showing what the product/service can do for someone.

The second technique is Pure Emotion Headlines.

These headlines focus on the emotional benefit a product/service has.

They're great for connecting with readers and making them feel something.

The third technique is Combined Benefit/Emotion Headlines.

These headlines show the main benefit of a product/service, and also the emotional benefit it has.

They're great for showing the benefits of a product/service in a clear and emotional way.

And as you've probably guessed, using the combined approach typically works best.

Tip 20 -

As a marketer, you want to make your campaigns better and talk to your audience in a way they understand.

One tool that can help you do this is ChatGPT.

It's an AI tool that makes text sound like it was written by a person.

Using ChatGPT can help you make your social media posts, emails, and chatbot talks more interesting and sound like they're coming from a real person.

It can also help you understand and talk to your customers in a way that makes sense to them.

Another cool thing about ChatGPT is that it can make things faster for you.

It can help you come up with new ideas for campaigns and write things like emails and social media posts.

Overall, ChatGPT and other AI tools are really helpful for marketers.

They can make your campaigns better and make it easier to talk to your customers.

If you want to make your marketing work even better, try using these tools as your unfair advantage in the marketplace.

BONUS SECTION: How To Write A Sales Letter/Video Sales Letter In 13 Simple Steps

The 13 Steps:

1 - Attention
2- Problem
3- Solution
4- Credentials
5- Benefits
6- Testimonials
7- Present Offer
8- Guarantee
9- Scarcity
10- Reason To ACT NOW
11- Final Reminder of What They Get
12- Final Warning About Scarcity/Urgency
13- Frequently Asked Questions

In this *tactical* section, what I'm going to be showing you is what works best for writing sales pages and video sales letters, as well as the most critical elements you must incorporate.

The first step is you've got to gain attention.

If nobody knows you, no one is going to buy from you.

For example, a lot of times you'll see in some advertisements, whether it's on Facebook or on a sales page say, "Attention business owners," or "Attention women who are 35 years and older," or whatever it might be, they're trying to grab the reader/viewers attention in a very direct manner.

If somebody is scrolling through their Facebook feed, you need them to stop and actually pay attention to what you're going to say because right now, you're interrupting their day, right?

They probably aren't looking at your stuff, right?

They're not trying to find your ad.

They're just looking at their friends' profiles and doing stuff and boom, there comes your ad, right?

So you've got to gain attention with a killer picture *first* and then with some killer copy.

Listen, your first job is to grab their attention.

Think of it like grabbing them by the shirt collar and being like, "Hey, come here buddy.

I have something to tell you."

So step one is to gain attention.

Now, after you've done that, you've got to figure out what the biggest problem is for your prospect.

When you do this, there's tons of ways you can find it.

I'll reveal a secret I learned from Jay Abraham that lets you find out what their biggest problems are.

I'm not a big fan of focus groups.

That's a very old school way of doing things.

And frankly, what people say and how they behave are two completely different things.

So I like to use a couple simple research tactics.

The first one is to go on Amazon and look up the niche you're writing for, let's say you're in the weight loss niche and you're trying to sell some kind of e-book, or physical supplements, or whatever it might be.

You're going to type weight loss keywords in the search bar to find tons of books.

And then you're going to go ahead and sort through the top 100 books, and you're going to grab all of the best five star reviews.

After that, you're going to look for books that have thousands of reviews or DVD programs or whatever it might be.

And what you want to do is identify what these people loved about that particular program.

Generally, when someone leaves five star reviews, they really love the product and they'll actually explain and tell you what problems they were overcoming

So you identify the problem because they'll tell you what it is in their review.

You're literally tapping into your prospect's mind just by being there and just by reading those comments.

Now, what you want to do is take those one and two star reviews, and then with those reviews you can turn those into bullet points, into benefits.

So if a review says, "Man, I hated this because it didn't show X, Y, and Z", then you just need to make sure that for your product, you show X, Y and Z.

Make sense?

Now, another secret tactic that you can use is go on Facebook and type in those same keywords you typed on Amazon.

You can literally just type on Facebook, "Struggling to lose weight," and it's going to pop up conversations that people were having publicly just posting on their wall.

And then what you want to do is, once you've got those stories, you want to really make them feel the pain in your copy.

You want to rub salt into the wound, so to speak.

And because you did the research, you'll have compelling stories that resonate with your audience, kinda like, "Hey, you know what? I've been in your shoes. I know what it's like to have this problem. Here's what I hated about it."

It can be a very emotional experience for the reader/viewer, once you've identified the problem.

Now that you've brought up the actual problem and added salt to the wound, now you want to give them the answer, which is your big solution, which is A.K.A., you, your product or whatever you're selling.

In every step, you will always want to paint the picture of what's happening and back it up with a story, even if it's a little bit small story.

Stories really help resonate your message with the intended recipient.

It also shows them that there's a light at the end of the tunnel and that you know what it's like to be in their shoes.

This kind of copy flow sucks the target in.

You've rubbed salt into the wound.

You've gotten them emotionally charged.

And now that they're feeling all this pain, and they're like, "Man, what am I gonna do?"

So, you identify the problem, and show that there's a solution.

And the solution you're promising is what's going keep them listening.

Make sense?

Now, why should they listen to you?

Because once you've given them the solution, they're automatically going to be a little skeptical, or they're gonna be like, "Who is this person? Why should I even listen to them? Are they just talking to talk? Or are they walking the walk?"

What you want to do here is, very briefly, state your credentials, your achievements, anything that's going to position you as an expert.

If you're selling some kind of financial advice, then showing how the expert has successfully predicted past stocks is a great way to establish credibility.

You don't have to have been a college graduate to present yourself as an expert.

You can say, "I've written over 20,000 articles or 1500 articles on this particular subject.

I've been featured in this magazine.

I've done this, that, whatever.

And I've been in the game and I know what works, what doesn't work, etcetera."

The credibility section is generally short, very to the point.

Now, what are the benefits?

So after you've shown them, "Hey, I'm the expert, I'm the "doctor" of the situation.

I'm here to diagnose your problems and give you the solution."

Now you're going to say, "Here are the benefits of the solution I'm providing.

I provide this magic pill for you as the doctor, and here are the benefits of this pill."

Now, the benefits, if you're doing a sales letter or video sales letter, think of them like bullet points.

It doesn't necessarily have to be bullet points, but it's probably the easiest way to describe it, especially if you're totally new.

And so, one of the ways I like to do it is, have the feature of your product, and then back it up with the benefit of that product.

For example:

How To Throw A Punch *<Feature>*
So you never fear another man again *<Benefit>*

Full Bullet:

- **How To Throw A Punch -** So you never fear another man again...

Now, a lot of people confuse a feature and a benefit.

So here's another example for a feature...
"The light bulb is bright."

It's just describing what the light bulb is, it's bright. Very cool.

Why is that important?

Well, the benefit is, "that means you'll never have to light a candle again to light up your room".

Right?

So all the people back in the days before light bulbs, this was humongous, because they were probably like, "What the heck is a light bulb? Why do I want this?"

Then the benefit would be…

"Well, you'll never have to light a candle again. It will light up your room like magic."

The *pre-light bulb* buyer then would say... "Oh, that's pretty cool, let me test it out!"

Onward…

Do other people recommend you?

Think of these like testimonials (because many times they are exactly that).

After you've painted the picture of all the benefits and how you're gonna help your potential buyer, they're going to be hopeful, but they're also going to be skeptical because chances are, they've also been promised this very same stuff before and other people have let them down.

So you want to overcome that.

But you can't overcome that by just saying, "Hey, I'm an expert."

No one's gonna listen to you.

So to overcome that, you let other people do the heavy lifting. You let other people say how great you are.

Because then it's not bragging, then it's just customer feedback, right?

So overcome their skepticism with testimonials and feedback from previous customers or clients.

Now, let's say you have zero customers and zero clients.

Well, let's be honest here, it's not *that* difficult to get a testimonial.

I'm sure you've got 10 of your friends that you could give your product to in exchange for a cool testimonial based on their experience, right?

Of course you can!

So this doesn't have to be crazy hard.

You can do this right from the get go.

I mean, if you don't have 5 to 10 people to give your product to, you've got to find 5 or 10 people.

Just sell something you really love and you'll find 5 or 10 people to show it to pretty quickly.

You'll go to the beach, or the mall, or walk around wherever you live and say, "Hey, check this out, man.

If you like it, do you mind if I shoot a video of you telling me your experience with it?"

They'll say…

"Yeah, that sounds cool."

And then you reply with...

"Okay, sweet. Thank you, man. Here, check it out."

Simple, right?

Listen, there shouldn't be any excuses. You've got to get testimonials.

Whether you've got them already or you need to generate them, you've got to have them in your arsenal.

After you've presented your credentials, demonstrated the benefits, overcome their objections and their skepticism with the testimonials...

... Now you're going to present them with a killer offer.

And you want to make sure that this offer is pretty much impossible to refuse.

As the famous copywriting saying goes... it needs to be "irresistible".

And here's what that means, it's like if I were going to sell a Ferrari and instead of it being $120,000, I would give it to you for $30,000.

That is an amazingly, crazy, ridiculous offer, right?

So it is an offer that makes your reader/viewer say, "oh my goodness, this is unbelievable."

And then since it is so unbelievable, you'll have to overcome their skepticism some more with testimonials.

That example really illustrates my point.

It's got to be a super irresistible deal where it seems like a no-brainer.

Now, the reason for that is because if you've got a killer offer, an offer that's just amazing, mind-bogglingly great, it will overcome weak copy.

So if you're not the best copywriter and you don't have the money to hire a copywriter to write one of these for $10,000+ for you, then that's totally cool. But make sure you've got a **killer offer because a killer offer will overcome weak copy**, but amazing copy **will not** overcome a weak offer.

You simply won't get sales if your offer sucks. So focus a great deal on making that offer completely irresistible and a total no-brainer decision, okay?

After you've done that, you'll want to give a guarantee.

Why do you want to do this?

Simple.

Because again, a little bit of skepticism might pop up just before they want to make a decision.

You overcame their skepticism earlier in your sales letter or video sales letter, but now that we're coming to the close, there's a good chance they're having last minute resistance and thinking, "That's an amazing deal.

Is this real?

This might be a scam or something.

This is insane."

Here's how you take away all of the risks to put their mind at ease. You give them a guarantee, a 30 day guarantee, a 60 day guarantee, whatever it might be.

Now, here's a quick tip.

If you're selling a high priced service or a high priced product, and when I say "high priced", I'm saying like $5000 or $10,000 or more, the longer the guarantee, so like a *365 day, one year money-back guarantee*, the better the customer, the easier of a sale you'll make, and the less refunds because they'll forget about the money-back guarantee since it's so far away.

If you used a 7-day money back guarantee for example, they'll mark it on their calendars and make sure they get their refund.

Either way though, you can definitely do a 30 day and still do a 60 day.

I'm not saying that everybody needs to do a one year guarantee, but it's just something to keep in the back of your head.

Interesting psychology there, right?

So, always give a guarantee. It's going to remove all of the risk from the buying decision for them.

Once you've done that, you're going to need to give them a reason to respond now.

One way is using scarcity.

You need to figure out if you're going to have a limited amount of whatever you're offering, or if your irresistible offer is going to expire on a certain date.

Whatever it might be, you've got to get it down.

Because if you don't have this, as the old saying goes, "delay is the death of a sale" and it's absolutely true.

If people have gotten to your pitch, they've read through it, or listened to it, or however they've consumed your pitch, once they're at the point where now it's about time to buy, a lot of people will just say, "Okay. Well, that's pretty cool.

Let me just take my time and I'll think about it, and maybe I'll come back tomorrow to buy it," or they'll tell themselves, "I've got so much stuff going on. I'm driving in the car. I'll buy it when I get to the house."

And then they'll forget about it forever.

You've got to give them a reason to act right now.

Most of the people who will see your message are going to be on their phone, you should remember that.

Here's what you want them to feel, "Oh my goodness, I'm driving. I've got to get this now though.

Let me pull over to the side of the road real quick, risk a ticket or something, and order this real fast."

That's what you want them to feel. That's what you're trying to get at.

So get that into your mind and then use that to really write your scarcity part because that's going to be huge in getting them to pay.

So after you've done that, you need to give them a reason to take action.

You've done that to a degree, but now you've got to tell them exactly how to order.

See, once you've removed the risk and injected the scarcity, you need to clearly ask for the sale.

You want to paint the picture, and when I say that here's what I mean...

If you're doing a sales page, for example, you can just say, "Click the button below right now to order," or, "Call this number, this number, and order immediately."

But what you don't want to do is end it on just, "Okay, so order today."

Something like that isn't going to fly as well as if you tell them <u>exactly</u> what to do.

When you say, click the button below that says, "Yes, I want my package," it's very specific in what they have to do.

<u>That's what you're aiming for.</u>

Another tip is to clearly describe what they're going to see on the next page and the page after.

So once you say, "Hey, click here to order, after you do you'll be taken to another page that will look like this..."

Then you can even insert a screenshot of what they next page will look like.

So what that does is it walks them through the buying process, step-by-step.

So when they click the button from one page and go to your order page, it's not something that they haven't seen before.

They were prepped and pre-framed that, "Okay, now I'm on this page. The next step he said is to fill out my billing details. And then the next step is I get my product or service," or whatever it is.

When you paint the picture and you actually describe what the future steps will be, it helps boost your conversions like crazy.

Now, what happens if they don't order?

Oh, no.

Okay, so when this happens, it's actually pretty simple because you're identifying it.

You're actually painting the picture of what would happen if they *didn't* order.

You're saying, "Hey, if you don't take action today, here's what's going to happen.

Nothing's going to change. Your bank account isn't going to increase, blah blah blah."

You paint the picture and you bring back that original problem and say, "You don't want this in your life, right? I've got a solution. Here it is. Let's get rolling."

And then you bring them to a call to action again. But you want to paint the picture of all the bad things that can happen to them if they don't take action immediately.

After you've done all this, then you want to give them a final little reminder.

This is where you give them the last push over the edge to get them to buy.

You want to remind them of the features and benefits.

You're not necessarily going to go through all of them again... You don't have to put all 50 bullets or whatever you may have put before, but you want to narrow down the best ones that you can absolutely get and just put them in here.

For example...

"Here's a quick reminder of some of the things that you're gonna get and much, much more."

Then, you want thank them for their order because not enough people actually THANK their customers, right?

Not enough people show appreciation, and what everybody wants is to be appreciated, isn't it funny?

So one of the things that you can do is, after you go ahead and remind them of the features and the benefits, you thank them for the order.

And this is essentially when you thank them for the order, you're thanking them before they've clicked the button to order.

But what it does is it assumes the sale, just like that good ol' sales psychology, and it subtly pushes the prospect to want to buy.

It's kind of like implanting this thought in their heads... "Hey, thanks again for your order." They're going be like, "Oh, I haven't even ordered yet. I better do that."

And then after that, you remind them of the scarcity so that now they realize they need to take fast action and secure their order.

Because if they don't they could miss out!

Here's an example:

"Thanks for your order. I appreciate your business, make sure you take action right now because remember, you've only got the next 48 hours to take advantage of my crazy, killer deal.

After that, you'll have to pay full price, you don't want to do that. Let's take action right now. Pull over to the side of the road if you're driving and click here, even if it's 3:00 AM. Make sure you do this right now. Click the button below ASAP!"

Do you see how I'm going for the throat? I'm really trying to close the sale and I remind them when I push that scarcity. Now, the final section of your sales letter or video sales letter is the 13th step.

This is where I like to show the Frequently Asked Questions.

So what you want to do is gather a list of the 10 frequently asked questions regarding your offer and then you want to list them out.

Think of this final step at the bottom of the page as your "objection obliterators" where you're identifying any last questions lurking in the back of their head that might be preventing them from buying. You're identifying their questions and then you're going to answer them.

For example...

Question 1: Is this guaranteed?
Answer: Yes, absolutely. We fully backup all of our products with a 60 day guarantee. We want to make sure we're there for our customers and they're 100% happy with their product. So make sure you click here to order.

As you can see, I'm adding mini call to actions in each one of the answers to those questions.

So that's the final objection obliterator.

And then at the bottom of that is where you add another call to action button to encourage the sale.

You've Reached The Finish Line!

You've reached the end of this book, but your journey doesn't need to stop here.

Let me explain...

This book was not written by me.

At least... not entirely.

See, I took my thoughts, ideas, formulas and strategies and dumped it all into ChatGPT.

Like I mentioned in Tip 20 - ChatGPT is a language model developed by OpenAI.

It uses deep learning techniques to generate human-like text based on the input it receives.

And yes, it is AI.

If you'd like to learn more about how to use artificial intelligence by harnessing the power of ChatGPT...

...visit my website and I'll show you exactly how I'm using it in my own marketing and how you can use it too!

Here's the website:

AiCopywritingSecrets.org

Thank you again for snagging up this book.

Now go check out my website before something else pops up and distracts you.

I'll see you in the members area!

All The Best,

Carlos Redlich - Galindo

www.ingramcontent.com/pod-product-compliance
Lightning Source LLC
Chambersburg PA
CBHW070305220526
45465CB00004B/1755